GET A LIFE THAT DOESN'T SUCK

10 Surefire Ways to Live Life and Love the Ride

Michelle DeAngelis

RODALE

A Note to the Reader

All of the names of people used in the stories in this book have been changed, unless those people gave me permission to use their names or I state otherwise. In a few instances, composite stories were used from client material that was similar. In all cases the stories reflect the ideas and experiences of the people discussed.

Rodale books may be purchased for business or promotional use or for special sales. For information, please write to:
Special Markets Department, Rodale Inc., 733 Third Avenue, New York, NY 10017

Printed in the United States of America

Rodale Inc. makes every effort to use acid-free ♾, recycled paper ♻.

Photo credits: page 2, © Michael Blann/Digital Vision/Getty Images; page 28, © Jeremy Maude/Digital Vision/Getty Images; page 48, © Sean Locke/Photodisc/Getty Images; page 68, © Dimitri Vervitsiotis/Photographer's Choice/Getty Images; page 88, © Dimitri Vervitsiotis/Digital Vision/Getty Images; pages 102, 182, 214, © Stockbyte/Getty Images; page 122, © Photodisc/Getty Images; page 142, © Henrik Weis/Photodisc/Getty Images; page 160, © Photos.com; page 198, © flashfilm/Digital Vision/Getty Images; page 232, © George Doyle/Stockbyte/Getty Images; page 250, © Michele Constantini/PhotoAlto/Getty Images

Interior design by Joanna Williams

Library of Congress Cataloging-in-Publication Data

DeAngelis, Michelle.
    Get a life that doesn't suck : 10 surefire ways to live life and love the ride / Michelle DeAngelis.
        p.   cm.
    Includes bibliographical references and index.
    ISBN-13 978–1–59486–798–9 hardcover
    ISBN-10 1–59486–798–4 hardcover
    1. Success—Psychological aspects.   2. Self-actualization (Psychology)   I. Title.
BF637.S8D366   2008
158—dc22   2008028336

Distributed to the trade by Macmillan

2   4   6   8   10   9   7   5   3   1   hardcover

RODALE
LIVE YOUR WHOLE LIFE™

We inspire and enable people to improve their lives and the world around them
For more of our products visit **rodalestore.com** or call 800-848-4735

To Joyce and Dean—
for being such living examples of joy.

To Babo—
for being my greatest teacher.

CONTENTS

PART THREE:
HOW TO ENJOY THE RIDE OF YOUR LIFE

WHY I WROTE THIS BOOK

Life can really suck.

Six years ago my mom was diagnosed with brain cancer, and she died just 34 days later. This was a cancer that doubled in size every seven days, so we knew she didn't have long to live. It was imperative for me personally, and for my family, to *enjoy* the little bit of time we had left with her. So I made a conscious decision to be fully present and drink in the last bit of my mom's existence. I chose to relish the time we had left as the gift that it was, Frankenstein scar and all. Her death was not about me, or my sadness, or how unfair it all was. It sucked, all right, but she wanted her death to be a continuation of her celebration of life—all the way to the end. So we were all there to hold her hand, reminisce with her, listen to her hallucinations, write down her words, give her morphine, crawl in bed with her, and give her as much comfort as possible. It was all about her.

Now, this was not to deny my own feelings. Sometimes I cried so hard the snot ran down my chin. No, this was feeling *all* of it, every bit. I wasn't worrying about what would happen after she was dead or cursing God for taking her too soon. That would have distracted me from her. I was just being. Showing up. Zooming out to see the beauty of her spirit and zooming back in to caress it. It wasn't feeling my own mortality; it was understanding the peace in death. It was an honoring time, a reverent time, a joyful time. In spite of it all.

It was one of the times I felt closest to that Universal Spirit that some people call God. I've had countless experiences where I was aware of Spirit, but none really quite like that.

One night I was sitting with my mom after she had lapsed into unconsciousness. I stayed close while the hospice staff rolled her over and back in her bed. She heaved a big, unconscious sigh. I'm not sure if she had any awareness at all, but I knew those sighs were big, weighty releases. Of everything. She was about to leave and go off to glory. So I sat there with my back against the headboard and her head in my lap. My dad held her hand and stroked her arm. She looked so peaceful. Her hair was straight and slicked back—she would have hated it—and she was not wearing makeup, after a lifetime of putting on her glamorous "face." Her skin was amazingly smooth and luminous, kind of freaky really. She seemed to be getting younger somehow, even as her organs shut down.

After a life of big bangs and so much larger-than-life hoopla, she let out her last bit of air in a quiet little whimper. The ultimate anticlimax. Her quiet coda.

And then she was gone.

One of her parting gifts to me was the absolute resolve to *truly live* every day.

I know people die every day.

I want people to LIVE every day.

And that's why I wrote this book.

INTRODUCTION

Two years ago I was sitting on the beach in Cabo, drinking a margarita and scribbling ideas for this book, when the guy on the beach chair in front of me asked, "Are you an author?"

"I'm about to be," I said. "I'm writing a book."

"What's your book about?" he asked.

I didn't really feel like chatting and the margarita had me a little feisty, so I ran through my mental shorthand of what my book is *really* about and said, "It's about how to get a life that doesn't suck."

"Oh my god!" he said. "I know 20 people who need that book!"

Oh my god is right. Those words were just what I needed to hear. Finally, I had learned to describe my book so people would actually want to read it.

You see, until I figured out how to get that response, I dreaded answering the question "What's your book about?" I had learned what *not* to say, that's for sure. I couldn't say to the skeptics and the jaded who were posing as innocent inquirers, "It's about raising the level of joy on the planet by showing people how to create joy in their lives every day, no matter what." Oh hell no. When I said that, all they could see was a saccharine swirl of pixies, unicorns, and fairy dust dancing around my head. *Joy schmoy.* Each time I started up with that little ditty, I got responses ranging from a polite "Oh, really?" to one guy who looked at me like I was the first brunette with three heads he'd ever seen.

So I learned I had to cross over to the dark side.

I had to morph from Mary Poppins into Darth Vader. No spoonful of sugar was helping the medicine go down. I had to cross over from the *happy* place where I live to the *crappy* place where many other people live. It was like that great scene in *The Wizard of Oz* when Dorothy steps from her black-and-white farmhouse into the amazingly colorful world of Oz. Only in reverse. And no, I wasn't in Kansas anymore.

Actually, those hundreds of excruciating "What's your book about?" dialogues had been great market research. They told me several things. First, there was a disconnect between what I had to say and how people could hear it. I had to change my approach especially when coaching. No more asking people to come over and join me at the joy place, no sirree. I had to go to them. I had to meet people in their misery, spend some time with them there, and then, once they felt heard, lob out a couple of casually phrased suggestions about taking responsibility and making good choices. And make it all sound possible. Oh, and worthwhile.

Second, I learned that the word "joy" had become code for something to be disbelieved. Something magical that's out of reach but still within sight and blinking with a tormenting "Neener, neener, you're a jerk for even attempting to be happy, sucker." I definitely could not lead with the word "joy." It could only be uttered among believers, like some Skull and Bones ritual chant.

Third, I learned that people secretly hoped I was right. They were cranky and miserable and full of doubt, yet they hoped against hope that I could find a vein and inject some kind of joy juju that would let them get rid of their pain and *believe* again. People want to be happy.

For everyone who is sick and tired of being sick and tired, *Get A Life That Doesn't Suck* offers a better way to live every day. It's street-smart wisdom served up with a heaping side dish of irreverence. If you are bored, numb, disenchanted, or in despair, this book is your antidote. It's about you waking the hell up and truly living. This book will show you how to thrive instead of just survive. And yes, pixies and fairy dust aside, it *is* about finding and creating joy in your life, every day, *using very specific tools and techniques.*

WHAT THIS BOOK DOES AND DOESN'T DO

This is not a scientific book. There are already a whole bunch of books out there on the science of happiness: how it improves your health, how the power of joy can transform your life, the amazing differences that positive thinking can make. Conclusive studies have already proven the benefits of happiness and measured its related behaviors (get the dog to climb over the wall, get the person to make a decision, quantify and rate people's moods). *These books legitimize and confirm the fact that being happy is good for you.* And thank god for that. Those guys already did the hard work for me! My sincere appreciation goes to those people who have advanced the cause of happiness.

This *is* a fun and meaty book. It is a book for people who are finally ready to do something different in order to get a different result. I'm going to ask you to take a long, hard look at your fine self as you go through it, so you can go to another level in your life, a level where joy arises naturally out of your every breath, thought, and action. You'll learn some very specific processes, as well as some new terms for getting a life that doesn't suck. Warning: These may seem simple—or even silly—but there is magic in them, a magic that you'll notice soon enough.

- @ **The Gap**. Your "Gap" is the measurable difference between your thoughts and your actions. It is also known as the place where misery lives. Your Gap points out how in or out of sync your behavior is with your professed beliefs. A big Gap means they're out of sync, which sucks.

- @ The **BACK Technique** is a fast-acting method for relieving suckiness, like a painkiller. Use it when you encounter problems to get BACK on track. It takes just a few seconds to do and makes a huge difference.

- @ **Joyriding** is a way of living with your thoughts and actions aligned *so that you have no Gap.* You're in sync. Joyriding is a fun, kick-ass way to make sure you are living by the 10 Life-Changing Ahas and getting BACK to joy every chance you get.

- ◉ The **10 Life-Changing Ahas** are 10 actions that gradually and consistently improve your life, like taking vitamins improves your health. The Ahas are *not* optional. They are "must dos," so use them every day.

- ◉ Your **Joy Quotient** is a score that measures your joy, like an IQ, only it's a JQ. It is based on the size of your Gap.

- ◉ **Joy It On.** This is a way of giving that lets you spread joy so other people's lives can suck less. You're a joy generator!

This book has three distinct parts that are designed to meet you where you are now, escort you through the transition to greater joy, and deliver you to the other side—where life really, truly doesn't suck.

Part One is Why Your Life Sucks. This section is all about increasing your *awareness* of and knowledge about how you live your life now. This is where you learn the technique that will get you BACK to joy and find out what your JQ is.

Part Two is The 10 Life-Changing Ahas. This section guides you through the *transformation* to begin living by the Ahas. The JQ Quiz, the Ahas, and the BACK technique are all designed to work together to give you consistent joy experiences at home, at work, and at play. I give you very specific exercises and techniques to help you do that.

Part Three is How to Enjoy the Ride of Your Life. This is where you get to enjoy *mastery*. Now that Joyriding is second nature to you, you will see the benefits show up in your daily life.

I have spent 20 years observing thousands of not-so-happy people while working as a management consultant, speaker, and coach to Fortune 500

companies. Thousands of people who are miserable and slogging through life with dead eyes and no sense of purpose. Thousands of people whose lives suck. Thousands of people who have no idea that there is another way to live, that they can, in fact, learn how to create a joyful existence for themselves, even in the midst of life's sad or trying circumstances.

Okay, so we're not fixing world hunger here, but we're fixing *your* hunger—for life, for the sense of being alive, for a day worth remembering.

By the time you finish this book, you will

- See yourself differently
- See situations differently
- Find you have more options than you knew existed
- Believe that a win/win is possible
- Discover how to choose your way out of destructive behavior
- See bad news or challenges as "good information"
- Know when it's time to quit, leave, or stop

So what's it like when you "wake up" to joy? How will you know? You'll have at least one completely joyful moment every day. You'll learn what makes you happy, what brings you down, what boosts your energy, what improves your outlook, what you need to let go of, and how to do that. You might even miss complaining.